Moe Moe Learns His 123s

by Kenya C. Henderson

DORRANCE PUBLISHING CO
EST. 1920
PITTSBURGH, PENNSYLVANIA 15238

Dorrance Publishing Co
585 Alpha Drive
Suite 103
Pittsburgh, PA 15238
Visit our website at *www.dorrancebookstore.com*

ISBN: 979-8-8860-4158-3
EISBN: 979-8-8860-4814-8

Moe Moe
Learns His 123s

SNIFF
SNIFF

1, One, Uno

One nose to smell.

ZZZ
ZZZ

2, Two, Dos

Two ears to hear.

3, Three, Tres

Three toys to play with.

MOE MOE

4, Four, Cuatro

Four treats to eat!

5, Five, Cinco

Five jumps of joy!

6, Six, Seis

Six licks of love.

7, Seven, Siete,

Seven bones stored away.

DAY CARE
DOGG
DAYCAR

8, Eight, Ocho,
Eight days away,
I love you please stay.

DOGGY
DAYCARE
DOGGY DAYCARE
MOE

9, Nine, Nueve,

Nine belly rubs

from me to you!

HAPPY BiRTHDAY

10, Ten, Diez,

Ten tricks for you to see!

www.ingramcontent.com/pod-product-compliance
Lightning Source LLC
Chambersburg PA
CBHW040904110726
48005CB00001B/193